STEAM!

Taming the River Monster

Written by Wim Coleman and Pat Perrin
Illustrated by Sue Todd

RED
CHAIR
·PRESS·

Please visit our website at **www.redchairpress.com** for more high-quality products for young readers.

 EDUCATORS: Find FREE lesson plans and a Readers' Theater script for this book at www.redchairpress.com/free-activities.

About the Authors

Wim Coleman and **Pat Perrin**
Coleman and Perrin, a husband and wife writing team, have written over 100 publications. For 13 years these former teachers lived in San Miguel de Allende, Mexico where they created and managed a scholarship program for at-risk youth.

The Runaway Train: Taming the River Monster

Publisher's Cataloging-In-Publication Data
(Prepared by The Donohue Group, Inc.)

Coleman, Wim.
    Steam! : taming the river monster / written by Wim Coleman and Pat Perrin ; illustrated by Sue Todd.

    pages : illustrations ; cm. -- (Setting the stage for fluency)

    Summary: In 1807, folks living along the Hudson River saw a strange fire-breathing monster churning the waters. The sight of Robert Fulton's Clermont created havoc on the shore and river. One of the on-lookers, a young Brenton Dixon, got a job aboard the steamboat and assisted Fulton and his crew. Brenton continued working on steamboats throughout their great pre-Civil War heyday.
    Interest age level: 009-012.
    Issued also as an ebook.
    Includes bibliographical references.
    ISBN: 978-1-939656-74-2 (library binding/hardcover)
    ISBN: 978-1-939656-75-9 (paperback)

    1. Steamboats--United States--History--Juvenile drama. 2. Pilots and pilotage--United States--History--Juvenile drama. 3. Steamboat workers--United States--History--Juvenile drama. 4. Steamboats--United States--History--Drama. 5. Pilots and pilotage--United States--History--Drama. 6. Steamboat workers--United States--History--Drama. 7. Children's plays, American. 8. Historical drama. I. Perrin, Pat. II. Todd, Sue. III. Title.

PS3553.O47448 S74 2015
(Fic)   2014944178

This series first published by:
Red Chair Press LLC   PO Box 333   South Egremont, MA 01258-0333

Printed in the United States of America

1 2 3 4 5 18 17 16 15 14

TABLE OF CONTENTS

INTRODUCTION

On August 17, 1807, people who lived along the Hudson River in New York state saw an amazing sight. Some described it "as a monster moving on the waters, defying the wind and tide, and breathing flames and smoke." Actually, it was an early steamboat, designed by American inventor Robert Fulton.

This play is narrated by a fictional steamboat pilot in 1857. He is remembering that historic journey fifty years after it happened. Some of the characters in this play were real people. These were Robert Fulton himself, Robert Livingston, Livingston's wife Mary, his niece Harriet, Captain Davis Hunt, and George Jackson. All the other characters are fictional. But the play is true in many ways. Fulton actually did stop early in the trip to adjust the paddlewheels. Other inventors did try to power steamboats with jets of water. And some boatmen on the Hudson really did try to wreck Fulton's steamboat.

Later, historians mistakenly wrote that Fulton's steamboat was named the Clermont. In its own time it was called the North River Steamboat of Clermont, or simply the North River. Its first voyage on the Hudson started a great new era in steamboat travel. The American writer Samuel L. Clemens (better known as Mark Twain) was a Mississippi steamboat pilot as a young man. Later in life, he remembered those days in his book *Life on the Mississippi*. "Your true pilot cares nothing about anything on earth but the river," he wrote, "and his pride in his occupation surpasses the pride of kings."

THE CAST OF CHARACTERS

Older Brenton, Brenton Dixon in 1857, age 63; a Mississippi steamboat pilot; narrator of the main story

Younger Brenton, age 13 in 1807 when the main story takes place

Amy Dixon, Brenton's younger sister, age 11

Mother, Brenton's mother, about age 25

Neighbors 1, 2, and 3

Captain Jeremy Hadfield

Robert R. Livingston, known as the "Chancellor," age 60

Robert Fulton, an American inventor, age 41

Mary Livingston, wife of Robert R. Livingston, age 55

Harriet Livingston, Robert Fulton's fiancée, age 23

George Jackson, the steamboat's engineer

Mr. Espy, a rival inventor

Davis Hunt, captain of the steamboat

Spectators 1, 2, and 3, who see the steamboat from the shore

Boatmen 1 and 2

Fishermen 1 and 2

Setting: Along the Hudson River in the State of New York; aboard the *North River,* a steamboat better known today as the *Clermont.*

Time: Narrated in 1857; the main story takes place in 1807.

PROLOGUE

Older Brenton: So you want to be a steamboat pilot, do you? Well, there's no life to match it. And this is quite a boat, isn't she? Some 700 tons, almost 300 feet long. Three decks, two great smoke stacks, huge paddlewheels on each side. And what a view here from the pilot house! It feels like you're in command of the whole Mississippi River. And how old are you? Nineteen or 20? A good age to start as a "cub" pilot. Believe it or not, I was only 13 when I became an **apprentice**. That was 50 years ago, along the Hudson River in New York state. I remember it well …

Amy: *(in Older Brenton's memory)* Mama, Brenton! It's the river monster!

Older Brenton: My poor little sister, Amy! How could she know what it really was …?

SCENE ONE

Older Brenton: That was a Tuesday in August of 1807. About noon, it was. Amy and I lived with our mama on a **bluff** high above the river. My father had died just the year before. So Mama sewed, cooked, and cleaned folks' homes to keep us alive. Mama and I were working in our little garden when Amy came running up …

Amy: It's the monster!

Mother: What monster?

Amy: The monster that lives in the river! He woke up! He's coming after us!

Older Brenton: We youngsters in those parts told a story about a river monster. We said he'd been sleeping for years, but one day he'd wake up. And he'd eat children! But I was older and knew better …

Younger Brenton: Amy, there's no such monster.

Amy: I saw him! My friends saw him too! He's swimming up the river! We all ran away!

Older Brenton: Amy hid inside the cottage. Mama pointed …

Mother: Brenton, look! Just over the bluff! Black smoke! Fire too!

Older Brenton: Sure enough, a thick **plume** of smoke poured skyward. Sparks and flames were in it too.

Younger Brenton: What *is* it?

Mother: Let's go see!

Older Brenton: Mama and I ran toward the bluff. Some neighbors were already there, staring out over the river. Then I saw the thing too. It really did look like a fire-breathing beast, splashing water as it swam toward us. And it made a whole lot of noise—rattling, banging, and chug-chug-chugging.

Neighbor 1: What on earth is it?

Neighbor 2: It looks like it's alive.

Neighbor 3: No, it's a boat of some kind.

Neighbor 1: What kind of boat pours out smoke?

Neighbor 2: And fire?

Neighbor 3: And look how fast it's moving against the river current!

Neighbor 1: Against the wind too!

Neighbor 2: It can't be a boat!

Neighbor 3: Impossible!

Older Brenton: The thing got closer, and we could all see it better.

Neighbor 1: Look there—it has two masts.

Neighbor 2: It's a boat all right. But no sails are raised!

Neighbor 3: What keeps it moving?

Neighbor 1: Those big wooden wheels on either side—they turn round and round.

Neighbor 2: They've got paddles on them, splashing away in the water.

Neighbor 3: And that thick iron pipe sprouting up in the middle …

Neighbor 1: That's where the smoke and fire come from.

Neighbor 2: That boat is driven by some kind of machine.

Neighbor 3: How many folks are aboard?

Neighbor 1: Looks like couple dozen on deck.

Neighbor 2: Maybe three dozen.

Neighbor 3: Look, it's headed right toward Clermont Manor.

Neighbor 1: It's going to dock there.

Neighbor 2: Who wants to go down for a look?

Older Brenton: Mama and I ran back to the house and fetched Amy. Then we hurried down the hill after the others.

Older Brenton: Clermont Manor was a fine old place, a huge home on acres and acres of ground. It had its own **wharf**. A crowd of villagers had gathered there to meet the boat. The crew was tying her to a dock.

Neighbor 1: Did you ever see such a boat?

Neighbor 2: Never in my born days!

Older Brenton: She was nothing like this floating palace we're aboard right now. She was much smaller. She had one fifteen-foot-tall smokestack and two little paddlewheels. Her engine was a crazy mix of rods and wheels. As I stood staring, I heard a familiar voice call out …

Captain Hadfield: It's Fulton's Folly, sure enough!

Older Brenton: Rough, broad-shouldered old Jeremy Hadfield stepped out of the crowd. He was the captain of the *Lynx*, a little scow sloop—a flat-bottom sailboat with one mast. The *Lynx* carried cargo from town to town along the Hudson—flour, grain, hay, lumber, furs, and the like. Cap'n Hadfield shook his head.

Captain Hadfield: I'd never have believed it if I hadn't seen it!

Younger Brenton: But what *is* she, Cap'n?

Captain Hadfield: A new kind of boat, powered by steam. I read about her in the paper. She left New York City yesterday, supposed to be on her way north to Albany. I never figured she'd make it even this far. But—who have we here?

Older Brenton: Down the **gangplank** came Robert Livingston and his wife, Mary. He was the owner of Clermont Manor. An amazing fellow. He'd signed the Declaration of Independence in 1776. He'd sworn in George Washington as our first president. And lately he'd helped work out the Louisiana Purchase with France. That made the United States twice as big as it had been before. He'd once been the Chancellor of New York state, sort of like its governor. So everybody just called him "Chancellor."

Captain Hadfield: So Chancellor—what were you doing aboard this thing?

Chancellor: Why, I'm its part owner.

Mary Livingston: My husband's money got it built.

Captain Hadfield: His money!

Older Brenton: A tall, thin, handsome man came down the gangplank.

Chancellor: Let me introduce everybody here to my business partner. The brilliant inventor, Robert Fulton.

Older Brenton: A young woman followed down the gangplank.

Harriet Livingston: May I join you?

Chancellor: And this is his lovely **fiancée**—my niece, Harriet.

Robert Fulton: Pleased to meet all of you.

Captain Hadfield: Fulton—the fool himself!

Mary Livingston: Now, now, Cap'n.

Harriet Livingston: Where are your manners, sir?

Captain Hadfield: Are you really planning to take this thing all the way to Albany?

Chancellor: We surely are.

Robert Fulton: We're stopping overnight at the Chancellor's place here.

Chancellor: *(laughing)* If that's all right with you, Cap'n.

Captain Hadfield: It's *not* all right. You get this monstrous thing off my river, y'hear?

Harriet Livingston: *Your* river?

Mary Livingston: We didn't know you owned it, Cap'n.

Captain Hadfield: I've got a better right to it to it than you folks. So does every honest sailor and fisherman. This thing is a **menace** to us all.

Older Brenton: As Hadfield stormed away, he snarled at me …

Captain Hadfield: Boy, you stay clear of this boat, if you know what's good for you.

Older Brenton: I took that threat seriously. You see, I was almost fourteen. And on my next birthday, I was set to join the *Lynx's* crew as cabin boy. I wasn't happy about it. The Cap'n was a mean man. But with my family so poor, I needed the job.

Robert Fulton: What's the matter with that fellow?

Harriet Livingston: What's got him so angry?

Chancellor: Oh, the Cap'n's just like that. Folks say it's from disappointment. He was a sailor on whaling ships when he was young. He wanted to captain a whaler himself. But he was passed over, never got a ship. He wound up here on this river, captain of a little scow.

Older Brenton: A man called out to me from the deck …

George Jackson: Hullo, young fellow! You look able-bodied. Would you care to do some work? I'll pay you a good day's wage.

Younger Brenton: Is it all right, Mama?

Mother: But the Cap'n said …

Younger Brenton: If we're lucky he won't find out.

Mother: Oh, Brenton, this boat looks dangerous.

Younger Brenton: I'll be careful.

Mama: All right, then. Watch yourself!

Robert Fulton: Come aboard, son.

SCENE THREE

Older Brenton: I walked up the gangplank with Mr. Fulton. The man who had called out to me shook my hand.

George Jackson: Welcome aboard. I'm George Jackson, an engineer. I'm in charge of this boat's workings. Mr. Fulton, you say you want some fixing done on the paddlewheels?

Robert Fulton: Right. On the way here from New York, I saw them straining. The paddles reach too far into the water. We should make the wheels smaller. Take all the paddles off, then put them back so they don't drag so much.

George Jackson: That'll keep us busy for the rest of today.

Older Brenton: Mr. Fulton joined the Chancellor and Mrs. Livingston at the mansion. I went right to work with Mr. Jackson and several crew members. As we worked, he told me about the engine …

George Jackson: It's simple, really. It burns pine wood, which boils water. The water turns into steam, which expands to cause pressure. The pressure moves the pistons, which turn the wheels. Yes, simple—and clever too!

Younger Brenton: What can you tell me about Mr. Fulton?

George Jackson: Oh, he's a fascinating chap. Spent quite a few years abroad, inventing things for both the French and English governments. Weapons mostly. Had an idea for a sort of bomb that swims through the water like a fish. He called it a "torpedo." He never got it working, but I'll bet someone will someday. And he built a boat that actually traveled underwater. Named it the *Nautilus*—a "submarine" he said it was.

Younger Brenton: Is this the first steam-powered boat?

George Jackson: A fellow named John Fitch made one some 20 years back. It used oars instead of a paddlewheel. And there have been a few others. Mr. Fulton built one back in France, and this is his first boat in America. A lot of folks call her "Fulton's Folly," but we have high hopes for her. Say, you're a hard-working young fellow. We could use a hand like you. Would you like to stay on with us?

SCENE FOUR

Older Brenton: At home over supper that night, I told Mama and my sister about Mr. Jackson's offer.

Mother: But you're already set to be Cap'n Hadfield's cabin boy.

Amy: And that monster still scares me.

Younger Brenton: It's not a monster, Amy.

Amy: But I heard folks say it's likely to explode.

Mother: Brenton! Is that true?

Younger Brenton: I don't think so, Mama.

Mother: Is it just for this one trip?

Younger Brenton: If all goes well, Mr. Jackson says she'll keep sailing the Hudson as a packet boat.

Mother: A packet boat?

Younger Brenton: That means she'll carry mail, cargo, and passengers.

Mother: I almost feel sorry for Cap'n Hadfield. With a boat like that on the Hudson, what will happen to his business? No wonder he's mad about it.

Amy: That Cap'n's always mad about something.

Younger Brenton: Steam is the future, Mama. It's already getting used in factories. It powers machines for spinning cotton and wool. And for weaving cloth. And grinding up grain into flour. Nobody knows what it'll get used for next. Maybe new kinds of travel, even on land. Carriages without horses—can you imagine? Steam will change everybody's lives, Mama. This is my chance to be part of history!

Amy: Besides, old Cap'n Hadfield's too mean to work for.

Mother: You seem to have your heart set on this new steamboat. When would you start?

Younger Brenton: Tomorrow morning. That's when she sets sail again for Albany.

Mother: Well, then. Let's pack up what you'll need for the trip.

Older Brenton: I showed up for work early the next morning. As I came on deck, a passenger was introducing himself to Mr. Fulton and the Chancellor.

Mr. Espy: Willis Espy, at your service.

Chancellor: What brings you aboard, Mr. Espy?

Mr. Espy: Curiosity. I'm an inventor like yourself, Mr. Fulton. I'm working on my own steam-powered vessel. But none of this paddle-wheel nonsense. Mine will be powered by a jet of water forced out by the engine.

Robert Fulton: It's been tried.

Mr. Espy: Not by me. My boat will succeed, as surely as this one will fail.

Robert Fulton: Ours, fail?

Chancellor: What makes you so sure?

Mr. Espy: You tell me. How long is she?

Robert Fulton: A hundred and fifty-six feet.

Mr. Espy: Too long. Her width?

Robert Fulton: Eighteen feet at her widest.

Mr. Espy: *Much* too narrow. Her weight?

Robert Fulton: A hundred eighty tons.

Mr. Espy: And the engine is—let me guess. Twenty-four horsepower?

Robert Fulton: Exactly.

Mr. Espy: Well, there you have it. A stick of a boat, almost too heavy to stay afloat, and not enough power to keep her moving. What's her name?

Chancellor: We haven't properly named her.

Mr. Espy: That's just as well. No name, and you won't grow too fond of her. Less heartbreak when you lose her.

Harriet Livingston: She's done pretty well so far.

Mary Livingston: People laughed at her back in New York.

Harriet Livingston: They didn't expect her to get off the dock.

Mr. Espy: So she's gone a hundred miles or so. You've been lucky. It's a good 40 miles yet to Albany. And then some hundred fifty miles back to New York. Impossible! You won't make it. The paddles will break, or the engine will fail. Worse yet, the boiler might explode.

Chancellor: Aren't you afraid of being blown to pieces like the rest of us?

Mr. Espy: Ah, but the satisfaction I'll feel! It will be worth it!

Older Brenton: There was plenty of hard work to do before we sailed. Mr. Jackson and I loaded wood for fuel. We oiled and cleaned the pistons. We filled the boiler with water and fired up the furnace. Then, at nine o'clock sharp, Captain Hunt called out …

Captain Hunt: Prepare to shove off!

Older Brenton: The engine chugged, making a terrific noise. I was standing near a **starboard** paddlewheel.

George Jackson: Lad, I'd get away from there if I were you.

Older Brenton: I stepped away, and just in time. As the paddlewheels started turning, they sprayed water across the deck.

George Jackson: *(laughing)* That's a problem Mr. Fulton hadn't reckoned on! We'll build covers for the wheels before the next trip.

Older Brenton: Just then …

Harriet Livingston: Look there!

Mary Livingston: Another boat, coming toward us!

Older Brenton: It was Cap'n Hadfield's scow sloop, the *Lynx*. She came alongside and the Cap'n called out from the deck …

Captain Hadfield: So you've joined their crew, have you, boy? Well, you'll never serve on my boat now!

Harriet Livingston: What's he doing?

Mary Livingston: He's racing us.

Chancellor: Let him try!

Older Brenton: We were heading straight upstream, against the current and into the wind. The *Lynx* couldn't keep up. Next to us, she almost seemed to be standing still. As she slipped behind, Cap'n Hadfield yelled …

Captain Hadfield: Fulton! Chancellor! Don't dare come back this way!

Scene Seven

Older Brenton: The steamboat kept chugging right up the Hudson. We created a stir along the way. Terrified fishermen rowed their boats away from us. People gathered on the shore to see us, then hurried away in fear. At five o'clock that afternoon, we came in sight of the town of Albany …

Captain Davis: Prepare to make land!

Mary Livingston: How have we done so far?

Older Brenton: The Chancellor looked at his pocket watch.

Chancellor: Superbly. We've made 40 miles in just eight hours.

Robert Fulton: That's a steady speed of five miles an hour.

Harriet Livingston: Amazing!

Older Brenton: We docked in Albany, and Mr. Jackson and I did some small repairs. We all rested that night, then set out again at nine o'clock the next morning.

Mary Livingston: Well, Mr. Espy, we've made the first half of our trip.

Harriet Livingston: What do you think of our boat now?

Mr. Espy: She's been lucky, I'll grant you that. But mark my words, that's sure to change.

Older Brenton: This time folks weren't so scared as we sailed by. People on the shore shook their fists at us …

Spectator 1: Such a racket!

Spectator 2: Such awful smoke!

Spectator 3: Keep that ugly thing clear of here!

Older Brenton: … and so did boatmen aboard sloops and scows.

Boatman 1: Get rid of that thing!

Boatman 2: You'll ruin our trade!

Older Brenton: This time, fishermen dared row near us …

Fisherman 1: You're scaring our fish!

Fisherman 2: You'll cost us a whole day's catch!

Older Brenton: Waves from our paddlewheels rocked their little boats …

Mary Livingston: Your boats are in danger!

Harriet Livingston: Go back, go back!

Older Brenton: … and they rowed away as fast as they'd come.

Fisherman 1: Blamed machine!

Fisherman 2: A menace!

Older Brenton: As for us …

Chancellor: We've got some hard work ahead, Fulton. The current is with us this way, but we're sailing into the wind again.

Robert Fulton: All the better to show her at her best.

SCENE EIGHT

Older Brenton: At six o'clock that evening, we neared Clermont Manor again. Just then …

George Jackson: Look there, off the starboard side!

Harriet Livingston: Why, it's that scow!

Mary Livingston: Cap'n Hadfield!

Chancellor: It's the *Lynx*, sure enough.

Robert Fulton: Is Hadfield trying to race us again?

Older Brenton: Mr. Espy was looking out over the rail, highly amused.

Mr. Espy: *(laughing)* Hardly that, my friends.

Older Brenton: The Cap'n stood on his deck, his face full of fury. The *Lynx* was coming straight at us.

Chancellor: He means to smash into the paddlewheel!

Mr. Espy: I'm afraid your luck has run out.

Harriet Livingston: But he'll wreck his own boat too.

Mary Livingston: Can he possibly be that angry?

Older Brenton: I knew the Cap'n well enough to be sure …

Younger Brenton: He really *is* that angry.

Older Brenton: Captain Davis called out to our pilot …

Captain Davis: Hard to **port**! As hard as you can turn her!

Older Brenton: Our steamboat **lurched** to one side, safely out of the *Lynx's* path. But Mr. Espy had been leaning a little too far over the rail, and …

Mr. Espy: Help! Help!

Harriet Livingston: Oh, no!

Mary Livingston: He's gone over the side!

Chancellor: And he can't swim!

SCENE NINE

George Jackson: Man overboard!

Captain Davis: Lower the lifeboat!

Older Brenton: But there was no time for that. Mr. Espy was sinking too fast. Now, I'd lived near the river all my life. And I'd saved a friend from drowning once before. So I knew what to do. I shook off my jacket, kicked off my shoes, and jumped over the rail. I swam as hard as I could toward Mr. Espy. His head barely bobbed above the water.

Mr. Espy: Help!

Younger Brenton: I'm coming!

Older Brenton: When I got to him, I turned my back toward him …

Younger Brenton: Stop splashing!

Older Brenton: … and pulled one of his arms over my shoulder …

Younger Brenton: Don't panic!

Older Brenton: … and his other arm around my side …

Younger Brenton: Don't choke me.

Older Brenton: … but he still kept thrashing …

Younger Brenton: Stop that! You'll drown us both!

Older Brenton: … and then he relaxed and let me carry him on my back.

Younger Brenton: That's better!

Older Brenton: I looked around …

Younger Brenton: The *Lynx*! Just a few feet away!

Older Brenton: I paddled to the scow. Cap'n Hadfield reached down from the deck to help us out of the water.

Captain Hadfield: Well done, boy. Well done.

Older Brenton: In another moment, Mr. Espy and I were safely aboard the *Lynx*. Mr. Espy looked shaken and embarrassed. He didn't have anything to say for himself. But the Cap'n did …

Captain Hadfield: Son, I behaved like a blamed idiot back there. I'm sorry.

Younger Brenton: I'm sorry too. Sorry that the steamboat is going to change your river.

Captain Hadfield: That it will, that it will. But progress is progress. There's no stopping the world from changing. I'll make do somehow. But you've got a great opportunity, son. You'll be a bigger fool than I not to make the most of it.

EPILOGUE

Older Brenton: We docked in New York City at four o'clock the next afternoon. Nobody there was laughing. And nobody was talking about "Fulton's Folly."

Chancellor: From New York City to Albany, then back again!

Robert Fulton: A hundred fifty miles!

Chancellor: And all in just 62 hours! No boat in the world can match that.

Older Brenton: The steamboat kept sailing the Hudson as a packet boat. I stayed on. And Mr. Fulton and the Chancellor gave her a name.

Robert Fulton: Let's call her the *North River Steamboat of Clermont*.

Chancellor: D'you mind if I just call her the *North River*?

Older Brenton: Many years later, a historian got her name wrong, wrote she was called the *Clermont*. Folks have called her that ever since. Then in 1811 …

Robert Fulton: Good news, Brenton. The Chancellor and I are launching a new boat on the Mississippi.

Chancellor: The *New Orleans*, she's called.

Robert Fulton: Want to come aboard?

Older Brenton: I did indeed. And for 50 years, I've watched the steamboat grow to be the river's glory. But it's not just rivers anymore. Long ago, Mr. Fulton predicted that great steamships would cross the oceans and bring all nations together in peace …

Robert Fulton: Freedom of the seas will be the happiness of the Earth!

Older Brenton: Well, not all has been happiness since then. But for good or bad, steamships do rule the oceans now. They link up all the continents of the world. Like Cap'n Hadfield said …

Captain Hadfield: There's no stopping the world from changing.

Older Brenton: Who can guess what changes *you'll* see in your lifetime, young fellow? What wonders might be right around the corner? Now go on and take the wheel of this fine boat. Let's see what you can do.

WORDS TO KNOW

apprentice: a person who is learning a trade from a skilled employer, having agreed to work for a fixed period at low wages

bluff: a steep cliff or bank

fiancée: a woman engaged to be married, wife-to-be

gangplank: a removable walkway used to board or leave a boat

lurched: made a sudden sideways movement

menace: something or someone likely to cause harm

plume: a long cloud of smoke shaped like a feather

port: the left side of a boat when you are facing forward

starboard: the right side of a boat when you are facing forward

wharf: a structure where boats can load and unload cargo or passengers

Learn More about Robert Fulton and Steamboats

Books:

Pierce, Morris A. *Robert Fulton and the Development of the Steamboat.* PowerKids Press, 2003.

Rebman, Renee C. *Robert Fulton's Steamboat.* Compass Point Books, 2008.

Zimmerman, Karl. *Steamboats: The Story of Lakers, Ferries, and Majestic Paddle-Wheelers.* Boyds Mills Press, 2007.

Web Sites:

Fulton's First Steamboat Voyage:
http://www.eyewitnesstohistory.com/fulton.htm

New York History: Fulton and The Clermont:
http://tinyurl.com/qhb2pp8

Places:

Robert Fulton Birthplace
Quarryville, Lancaster County, Pennsylvania